Natural Church Development 101

9780998702124

By **Christian A. Schwarz**
Revised by **Petr Cincala**

Natural Church Development 101

A pastor tells the story of a church to which he was assigned that had been experiencing a significant decline in membership–a trend that spanned several decades. The church had many obstacles standing in its way: a tiny congregation, small staff, and limited ministries. As the pastor surveyed the circumstances of his new congregation, he wondered if there was any way to revive this body of believers and become a beacon of hope to an ever-changing city.

The pastor's first task was to help the congregation realize the seriousness of the church's situation. The members needed to develop the realization that unless changes were made–and fast!–the days of the church were numbered. As the pastor sat with the church board and went over the statistics of decline that spanned the last 15-20 years, he saw an urgency develop in their faces. As they began to comprehend that the church had been on a downward trajectory for years, the severity of their situation dawned on them. It had taken years to get into their current predicament, and it would take something more than a "quick fix" to get them out of it. The board voted to make a long-term attempt at change by utilizing Natural Church Development (NCD) as a tool to help reverse their current downward trend.

Over the next seven years, the congregation took the NCD church survey multiple times to assess their health and growth. The profile showed scores on eight church qualities (empowering leadership, gift-based ministry, passionate spirituality, effective structures, inspiring worship services, holistic small groups, need-oriented evangelism, loving relationships), and allowed the church to compare their results from survey to survey. Church leadership discovered that things began to improve only once the majority of the members were intentionally aware of the church's weak areas and understood the need for creating a more healthy environment in which God could work.

Across the course of seven years, this congregation completed five cycles of the NCD process, and continued to experience not only dramatic, but lasting, change. The church became a vibrant body of believers; on their last NCD survey, their average score on the survey was well above a 65, indicating that the church was considered "healthy." In addition, the church planted a small congregation on the other side of the town. By taking an honest look at where they were, and developing a plan to change, this church experienced a growth in membership, weekly church attendance, and members' personal giving. Best of all, this group of believers was bringing others into the saving knowledge of Jesus Christ.[1]

You may be reading this story and wonder, "Sure it worked for them. But what about my church?" There's good news: the NCD principles can be applied to any Christian church, no matter its size or location.

---

[1] Mills, R. (2016). Healthy churches grow. *Journal of Applied Christian Leadership, 10*(2), 68–76.

→ Chris Hodges, pastor of Church of the Highlands[2] in Alabama, believes wholeheartedly in the validity of the NCD survey and results. He has been implementing NCD principles at his church since it's conception, always striving to increase their lowest factor and reach higher levels of health and vitality. Today, Church of the Highlands is the largest church in Alabama with an average weekly attendance of 48,434 as of 2018,[3] and is recognized as one of the largest megachurches in the entire United States.[4][5]

→ Jack Smith, pastor of City Place Church[6] in Columbia, Tennessee, has seen the value of the NCD process as he seeks to plant churches throughout small, rural towns in Tennessee. City Place was founded on three principles: the importance of an inspiring, God-centered environment, the centrality of relationships–specifically through small groups, and the call to multiplication. In September of 2017, Smith felt the Lord calling him to plant another church. Through the implementation of NCD principles and the structure already established at City Place, within nine months the church plant was in

---

2 https://www.churchofthehighlands.com

3 http://media.churchofthehighlands.com/special/legacy/2018_Highlands_Legacy_Report.pdf

4 Hartford Institute for Religious Research

5 For more thoughts from Hodges on NCD, watch this inspiring video:
https://vimeo.com/30397725

6 https://www.cityplacechurch.tv

motion; in August 2018, Sweetwater Church[7] launched in Culleoka, Tennessee.

→ John Kimball, Director of Church Development for the Conservative Congregational Christian Conference,[8] has used the NCD process in several ways to minister to his denomination as a whole. Kimball has used NCD as the primary assessment tool for their church revitalization work; additionally, the NCD process has also been used as the backbone of their specialized "directed development" work in the CCCC's Turning Point Initiative (which focuses on local congregations that find themselves in need of intensive evaluation and coaching). Within the CCCC, there has been a great success in addressing key issues and obstacles in most churches, setting them on a path towards greater health and fruit. Even congregations who find themselves in "critical condition" have benefited/improved by using the NCD process.

Just as Jesus asked the man sitting by the Pool of Bethesda, "Do you want to get well?" (John 5:6), the same could be asked of many churches today. Does your church want to "get well?" Does it realistically understand its strengths, as well as deficiencies and weaknesses? Does your church want to become a more vital body of believers? Do leaders and members alike want to bring souls into the Kingdom for the sake of Jesus Christ?

---

[7] http://www.sweetwater.church

[8] http://www.ccccusa.com

If this is your desire, then look no further, my friend. Natural Church Development 101 will give you the information you need to get started on the path to becoming a healthy, vital church.

Petr Cincala, NCD America Executive Director

Why do we have such a hard time with church growth?

Jesus uses the example of soil to illustrate the way the word of God reaches into people's lives and hearts (Matt. 13:1–23; Mark 4:1–20; Luke 8:4–15). Just as seed grows different in different kinds of soil, the Word of God reaches different types of people in different ways. However, it's important to remember that the seed itself does not do the growing; the environment of the growth–the soil–is what actually allows the seed to grow. Chris Hodges explains that "in our churches, we have to make sure that the culture–the soil–is healthy for healthy [practices] to work. And a lot of attention has to be given to the condition of [the] soil."

Have you ever observed a farmer begin preparing a new field for crops? He doesn't just go to his new piece of land and carelessly throw seeds out into the dirt, expecting a harvest in the fall. Instead, he begins by carefully plowing the land to ensure the seeds can fall on soft soil. He will take soil samples so he can figure out what elements are missing from the soil. Once he does that, he will add different supplements into the soil to compensate for what is already there. Only after he is certain the soil is ready does he carefully sow seeds.

Throughout the growing season, the farmer does not forget about his crops and simply hope they'll produce good fruit. He spends hours in the field, checking his seedlings to ensure they are growing well, providing water and fertilization where needed, ridding the field of weeds and pests that might destroy his crops. Producing a good harvest is hard work, but well worth it.

Christian Schwarz, the founder of NCD, uses the illustration of a cart with four square wheels transporting a load of wonderfully round and well-functioning wheels. When trying to move this cart, it would have to be pushed and pulled along; those attempting to move the cart would likely feel a great dedication to their task, yet their enterprise would move along extremely slowly and would prove to be quite a frustrating endeavor.

This picture is more than merely a caricature. In fact, it is an apt depiction of the widespread condition of many parts of the church of Jesus Christ. While the church experiences forward movement, everything happens slowly.

Why is this so? The illustration of the cart with square wheels reveals that the circumstances are not the real problem. Even if the conditions around the church were more favorable, the real problem would still exist.

The bottom line here is this: everything that we need to see the church grow has already been provided by God. The problem is that we do not make use of it. Instead of applying the principles (that is, utilizing the round wheels inside the cart) that God has given us, we try to push and pull the church in our own strength. We may even feel that the use of "square wheels" is linked to something particularly spiritual.

In order to begin forward movement, the "round wheels" that have been so abundantly provided in the church must be utilized and mounted where they belong according to God's plan. The Natural Church Development process helps a church uncover the round wheels that already exist in the church, and compels the church to put those wheels in place so it can experience smooth motion.

In this day and age, there are many factors working against the Christian faith in general. As Christians, we try to fit the gospel into our time and place, but our message is not a "hot seller" with much of today's society. Many churches lack relevance to the world today. The US NCD data shows that young adults tend to be the least present age group in churches but yes–you guess it–they prefer to be part of healthier and vital churches.

The NCD survey and related processes to improve low-scoring areas are similar to the work a farmer does on his field. First, an assessment must be taken to "sample the soil." Then, once the results are in, adjustments must be made based on deficiencies. However, the work does not stop there; ongoing assessment and cultivation of the seeds is necessary. Only then can the harvest be assured.

A Need for Proven Principles

Many church leaders today are focused on vitality and health rather than church growth, as an increasing number of churches are declining, if not dying. The focus of a number of denominational researchers is on finding a way to help churches get on the right track towards revitalization. Perhaps there is a suspicion towards research from the outside. However, the goal of NCD is not to present questionable research or management techniques, but simply to sharpen our perspective on the principles that God Himself uses to build His church. The more we deal with these principles, the more we learn about how God works among us, and the better we are able to reflect them in our Christian walk.

But how can we find out what these principles are? If you asked pastors of healthy, growing churches about the "secret of their success," you would hear many different answers. Some may feel that the secret to their success is a worship service that is geared toward Nones (those without any religion). Others are sure that the key to their growth is the centrality of worship and the nurturing of believers.

Others might praise their church's marketing methods as an essential approach to church growth, while others successfully expand their church without ever having considered the need to market their church.

It would be hard to determine a common denominator in all these answers. As convincing as each pastor's answer might sound by itself, each answer piled on top of the others only contributes to the confusion even more. Which answer is "right?" Also, when we hear the claim, "Do like we do, and you too will have the same success!" we really have only two options: either we fully buy into a model, or give up before we start.

Fortunately, there is a third option: instead of listening only to the leaders of these large growing churches, we can study the churches themselves to find out if there are common characteristics in all growing churches. Thus, instead of just learning from only one church, we can investigate literally thousands of model churches, both big and small. This allows us to uncover which of the elements studied are generally valid principles, and which elements are perhaps interesting, but not generally applicable elements of church growth.

It took me years to really understand this difference. Today, we refer to this as the difference between a "model-oriented" and a "principle-oriented" approach. "Models" are concepts that one or more churches have experienced positively; however, imitating these experiences may not at all be the right answer for churches in other situations. "Principles," however, are those broader practices that have been proven to apply to all growing churches around the globe.

What Growing Churches Do Differently

In the early 1990s, NCD International conducted research to establish a database large enough to come up with scientifically significant conclusions. Data from 1000 congregations on five continents was gathered: large and small churches, growing and declining ones, churches that faced persecution by the state and churches that were financially supported by the state, prominent mega-churches, as well as totally obscure ones.

Thus the most comprehensive research project ever on the topic of church development was conducted. Churches in 32 countries participated. The questionnaire, which has to be filled out by 30 church members in each church, had to be translated into 18 different languages. In the end, 4.2 million responses were analyzed.

This project led to extraordinary findings. For the first time, we had in black and white, right in front of us, principles that were proven to be universally used by God to build His church—literally from Alaska to Vladivostok, from Greenland to the Falkland Islands, from the North Cape to the Cape of Good Hope.

Since then, more than 75,000 churches worldwide have become involved with NCD. Ongoing research has helped sharpen NCD tools and has provided more clarity in how to apply NCD principles.

The Eight Quality Characteristics of Growing Churches

On the next few pages, we will examine the eight most important principles identified in the course of our study: empowering leadership, gift-based ministry, passionate spirituality, effective structures, inspiring worship, holistic small groups, need-oriented evangelism, and loving relationships. We call them the "eight quality characteristics of growing churches." While every church has the noun present (i.e. every church has leadership, ministry, spirituality, etc.), not every church possesses the adjective (i.e. empowering leadership, gift-based ministry, passionate spirituality, etc.). These adjectives are what make the difference between a struggling church and one that is healthy and vital.

When it comes to church life, there is no distinction between personal development and church development; we develop the church by developing people. We increase the quality of the church by increasing the quality of people. We facilitate the health of the church by facilitating the health of people.

There is no question that at first, this all sounds a bit theoretical. However, as soon as we take a look at what is hidden behind each one of these principles, you will notice that they have something to do with the condition of your own church. NCD research taught us that no church that wants to grow can neglect even a single one of these characteristics.

Quality Characteristic 1:
Empowering Leadership

> **❝**
>
> And he gave the apostles, the prophets, the evangelists, the shepherds and teachers, to equip the saints for the work of ministry, for building up the body of Christ, until we all attain to the unity of the faith and of the knowledge of the Son of God, to mature manhood, to the measure of the stature of the fullness of Christ.
>
> (Ephesians 4:11–13, ESV)

Please notice that our first quality characteristic is not called "empowered" but "empowering" leadership. Let me explain the difference. "Empowered leadership" could mean that there is one (sometimes several, but usually just one) ingenious, multi-gifted leader with a great vision; this type of leader always needs volunteers to help him turn his vision into reality.

Outside the Christian realm, this concept is sometimes known as "guru-leadership," but similar models can be found also in Christian churches. Some even defend this concept as an especially efficient expansion principle: here is the guru-leader with the great vision, there you have the lay troops who willingly serve their powerful leader to fulfill the his or her vision.

Our study shows, however, that this could not be farther from the truth. Leaders of growing churches do not try to build up their own power to become all-powerful. Leaders of growing churches consider that one of their most important tasks is to empower other believers (see 2 Timothy 2:23, 24). They equip, support, motivate, and mentor individuals to become all that God wants them to be–even if these empowered individuals are on a different trajectory than their leaders. However, empowering leaders can rejoice about such a Christian with all their heart because they know that God has a unique calling for every individual.

An interesting discovery made by the NCD survey is that pastors who reached the highest scores are hardly known to a wider public. Yet they provide more helpful basic principles of leadership than most of the world-famous spiritual "superstars." Leaders of growing churches do not have to be superstars. In fact, the superstar model can be a hindrance for church development. God generally does not fulfill His plans through super-gifted stars. If someone plays this role (or has to play this role because the church expects it), it is usually a sure sign that something is not going right in this church.

Quality Characteristic 2:
Gift-based Ministry

> **As each has received a gift, use it to serve one another, as good stewards of God's varied grace.**
>
> (1 Peter 4:10, ESV)

The conviction that God has already predetermined roles for each Christian in the church body is the basis for our second quality characteristic. Church leadership's role, then, is to help its members identify their gifts, then integrate those members into ministries that match their gifts (see Romans 12, 1 Corinthians 12:27, 14:1; Ephesians 4). This principle sounds quite simple, but its practical application will have enormous implications for all areas of church life.

When you live according to your spiritual giftedness, you are no longer working by your own strength; it is the Holy Spirit who works in you. Thus even though members are "just ordinary people," they can accomplish, in the true sense of the word, extraordinary things.

Knowing your gifts and not being able to put them into practice may be even more frustrating than not discovering them at all! Between 2008 and 2017, over a quarter of a million people were surveyed in the USA alone; of that number, only about half (51.5%) were certain about knowing their gifts, and felt that the tasks they perform in the church matched their gifts.

One of the interesting corollary results of NCD research was the discovery that no factor influences the sense of joy in living the Christian life more than if we are living it according to our spiritual gifts.

Quality Characteristic 3:
Passionate Spirituality

> **You shall love the LORD your God with all your heart and with all your soul and with all your might.**
>
> (Deuteronomy 6:5, ESV)

When considering a name for the third quality characteristic, we had to find a term that could describe the most divergent styles of spirituality. As far as the growth of the church is concerned, one result of our study indicated that the important thing (as long as spirituality is real) is not the way in which spirituality is expressed, but the fact that faith is actually lived out with commitment, fire, and enthusiasm (see Deuteronomy 4:29; Luke 24:32). The degree of spiritual passion is what sets growing churches apart from non-growing ones

This quality characteristic also illustrates that the methods a church employs are really a secondary concern. A church that lives out its faith with a passionate fervor will experience success with many different methods. In contrast, it is common that churches lacking in this area do not accomplish anything.

This characteristic ties in closely with living out a genuine Christianity. Only by approaching God according to your own spiritual style will your spirituality be authentic, and only authentic spirituality can be passionate.

Quality Characteristic 4:
Effective Structures

> **New wine must be put into fresh wineskins.**
>
> (Luke 5:38, ESV)

Interestingly enough, of all the eight qualities of growing churches, the "effective structures" quality characteristic has emerged as the most controversial. You might question, why would anyone hold to ineffective structures? The sad truth is that, in many churches, the model of the cart with the square wheels has become so normal that the use of square wheels is even seen as superior to the use of round wheels. However, it is important to understand that church structures are never an end in themselves, only a means to an end.

The most important criterion for structures is that they fulfill their purpose (see Acts 15:28; 1 Cor. 14:40); their purpose is to address growth in each of the three directions (upward, inward, and outward) and help to keep these three dimensions in balance. Whenever structures do not fulfill their purpose (for example, demeaning leadership structures, inconvenient worship service times, or programs that do not reach their audience effectively), those structures must be changed or laid to rest. Through this process of self-renewal, traditionalistic ruts can be avoided to a large extent.

So where does the resistance against this principle come from? Simply, it is the result of the lifetime tendency of people to become more and more traditional. "Traditionalism" means church forms have to stay the same way because "I have become used to them." It is not an accident that traditionalism is a factor that shows one of the highest significant negative correlations with church growth.

Quality Characteristic 5:
Inspiring Worship Service

> **"**
>
> When all the people of Israel saw the fire come down and the glory of the Lord on the temple, they bowed down with their faces to the ground on the pavement and worshiped and gave thanks to the Lord, saying, 'For he is good, for his steadfast love endures forever.'
>
> (2 Chronicles 7:3, ESV)

There is probably no other area of church life where the distinction between models and principles is so frequently violated as in the area of inspiring worship services. Countless Christians believe that they must adopt the worship models of other churches because these methods supposedly represent a formula for church growth.

However, NCD research indicates that the question is not whether our services target Christians or non-Christians, whether they celebrate "in the language of Canaan" or in a more secular language, or whether we worship using a liturgical or a free-flowing approach. Instead the key criterion is something else: Is the worship service an inspiring experience for those who attend it? (See John 4:23; Hebrews 12:28; Hebrews 13:15.)

The term inspiration comes from the term *inspiratio*, which literally means that the "Spirit flows into you." Because you have been inspired, you are able to inspire others. This inspiration allows people to connect both to God and to other fellow-believers in an intimate way.

Inspiring worship services are an area that clearly separates growing from non-growing churches. People who attend inspiring worship services unanimously declare that the church service is (and for some Christians this is almost a heretical word) "fun."

It is quite evident where most of the opposition to this quality characteristic comes from: Christians who attend the worship service to fulfill a Christian duty. They do not attend church because it is an experience that they would not want to miss for any reason; instead, these Christians attend to do God (or perhaps the pastor or a family member) a "favor." Some even believe that their "faithfulness" in patiently enduring an unpleasant exercise (i.e. an uninspired worship services) is blessed by God.

Quality Characteristic 6:
Holistic Small Groups

> **For where two or three are gathered in my name, there am I among them.**
>
> (Matthew 18:20, ESV)

Many growing churches have developed a system of small groups, allowing individuals to find intimate community, practical help, and intensive spiritual interaction. These are exactly the elements of the biblical concept of holism. In these groups, people do not only discuss Bible texts or listen to interesting explanations by experts, but also apply biblical insights to the everyday lives of participants. Holistic groups impact heads, hearts, and hands. Our minds are stimulated, our hearts are warmed, and our hands are activated so that we are eager and ready to change the world (see Acts 2:42–47).

In one of my seminars, I once shared the story of the world's largest church in Seoul, South Korea, which at that time had half a million members. One of the participants immediately responded that she could not even imagine becoming part of such a church. When I asked her why she felt that way she said, "Well, I could never stand the anonymity. I need the familiar atmosphere of people I know well."

Just a short time later, I actually met a pastor from that church and asked him how they deal with the problem of anonymity. He looked rather puzzled. "Anonymity?" he asked. "Nobody has ever complained about that in our church."

He then proceeded to tell me about how this church had developed a system of self-reliant cell groups of up to twelve members, and how most of the members of this church are integrated into this network.

NCD research shows that the principle on which this Korean church is based has universal validity. Christian small groups are not merely a nice, yet dispensable "passtime." No, they are the very essence of the true life of the church of Jesus Christ.

Quality Characteristic 7:
Need-oriented Evangelism

To the weak I became weak, that I might win the weak. I have become all things to all people, that by all means I might save some.

(1 Corinthians 9:22, ESV)

It does not take a worldwide research project to convince people that the mission of the church is inconceivable without evangelism. How else would the church fulfill its main purpose if not through the process of sharing the gospel?

As we conducted our survey, the question was not if evangelism was necessary; we wanted to determine if a correlation could be found between the practice of evangelism and the growth of the church. There are some who feel evangelism works best when you push people to commit their lives to Christ; many times, they do not even shy away from manipulative methods to reach this goal. It is no wonder many of us experience a strong gut reaction when we hear the word "evangelism."

However, for growing churches, evangelism is the most normal thing in the world. Their secret of sharing the gospel is that they do it in a way that meets the questions and needs of non-Christians (see Luke 19:9–10; Romans 5:8). They are able to look not just at evangelism, but at the whole church, through the eyes of non-believers; this allows them to better meet the needs of non-believers.

Quality Characteristic 8:
Loving Relationships

By this all people will know that you are my disciples, if you have love for one another.

(John 13:35, ESV)

I don't know how you feel about the term "loving relationships" but one thing is clear: growing churches manifest a measurably higher "love quotient" than stagnant or declining ones.

Whenever I use the expression "love quotient" in a seminar, there are always a few Christians who can't stand it. Love, according to a biblical understanding, is not just a warm feeling, but something that manifests itself in concrete actions (see 1 Thessalonians 3:12; 1 John 4:7–8). With this in mind, let me explain how we arrived at this "love quotient."

Our questionnaire contains a group of questions that allow us to determine how loving the relationships between Christians are. For instance, we ask if members find it easy to share their feelings with other Christians, if it is possible to talk about personal problems with people in their church, and if they feel they can rely on their friends at church. We ask if they experience joy and laughter in their church, if their church has an atmosphere influenced by words of praise and compliments, and if members can openly share their personal spiritual journey. We also ask if leadership shows concern for the personal problems of those in ministry and if leaders regularly praise/acknowledge volunteers.

All these questions impact the well-being of the church. Unfeigned, practical love endows a church with a much greater magnetic power than all the marketing efforts of this world. At best, marketing the church can be compared to artificial flowers; they may look deceptively real, but they have no fragrance. Real love, however, spreads a beautiful "aroma" that few can resist.

God's Principles

There are three things we can say about these principles today with a high degree of certainty: first, these are universally valid principles, meaning that they are applicable to churches around the globe; second, they can also be applied to our own context, meaning the results will look different from church to church; and third, each of these principles has a positive relationship with both the qualitative and quantitative growth of the church. If we are really concerned about reaching as many people as possible, we cannot afford to sacrifice any of these quality characteristics.

When it comes to numerical growth, there are spiritual, institutional, and contextual factors. We are not responsible for the contextual factors, but we are responsible for both the spiritual and the institutional factors. This is what the research reveals.

When we examine the eight principles more closely, some will be surprised to realize that each principle summarizes central aspects of the biblical message. How wonderful it is that NCD research confirms exactly what God has said in His Word!

The principles discussed in this brochure are nothing other than God's own principles. But please don't misunderstand: the terminology used in this book to designate the principles may not be perfect–like all scientific methodology–because they are the product of human beings. The books and resources we have developed can also be improved. However, all this does not change the fact that the principles, which we examined with our imperfect means and researched in our deficient ways, are God's own principles.

The "All-by-Itself Principle"

Here is the actual highpoint of NCD research: the principle that lies at the base of all eight quality characteristics is the so-called "all-by-itself principle." We have proof today that the secret to growing healthy churches does not consist in pushing or pulling the church with human strength and efforts. On the contrary, it is only through releasing our control and developing the potential God

Himself has laid into the church that growth can occur all by itself.

Simply put, church growth is something that we human beings cannot do. Our job is merely to releease the growth, allowing God Himself to build His church. So what does it mean?

This is not only a central biblical concept, but also applies to the practical work of the church. In Mark 4:26–29 (NIV) Jesus tells us the following parable: "This is what the kingdom of God is like. A man scatters seed on the ground. Night and day, whether he sleeps or gets up, the seed sprouts, and grows; though he does not know how. All by itself the soil produces grain–first the stalk, then the head, and then the full kernel in the head. As soon as the grain is ripe, he puts the sickle to it, because the harvest has come."

This parable shows explicitly what people can do and should do, and what they cannot do. They should sow and harvest; they may sleep and rise. What they cannot do, however, is bring about the fruit. Only God is able to do that. In this text, we find the mysterious description of the earth producing fruit "all by itself."

The Greek text uses the term *automate*–literally translated, it means "automatically." Thus, this passage explicitly speaks of a growth automatism. This is an important fact to consider. To the contrary of what some may think, this is a biblical concept (particularly according to the original text of the Bible).

This parable is not merely a nice illustration. No, it describes the very essence of church growth. Growing churches utilize this growth automatism, some deliberately, some intuitively. It is the "secret of their success!"

So how does such growth happen? To answer this question, one must simply review the verbiage of the eight quality characteristics. Each quality characteristic consists of two parts: a noun (e.g., leadership, ministry, spirituality, structures) and an adjective (e.g., empowering, gift-based, passionate, effective). The secret of each of these quality characteristics is not described by the nouns; every church has some kind of leadership, ministries, spirituality, or structures. Rather the secret is hidden in the practical application of what each of the adjectives represents.

A closer look at these adjectives reveals that they have something to do with making room for those growth automatisms God uses to build up His church.

Our Key Concern: The Quality of Our Churches

I don't know if what I have shared is something new for you, or if it is merely confirming something you already suspected or knew. For many Christians, these principles differ drastically from their ideas about "church growth" or "church development." One of the most important conclusions coming from NCD research is the insight that, whenever we think about the subject of church growth, the key is the quality of the church. Quality (as measured in the form of the eight quality characteristics) is the root; quantity (that is, vitality, demonstrated through increased church attendance, expanded member involvement, greater member giving, etc.) is the fruit.

This perspective has important implications for the practical work of the church. Instead of starting with the question: "How can more people come to our church?" we ask: "How can we grow in each of the eight quality areas?" Behind this approach is the theologically and empirically based conviction that quality in these areas will always impact quantitative growth.

Additionally, in today's society, people are concerned about how church will impact and/or transform their lives. A church that demonstrates a commitment to growth and health is typically one that is committed to the spiritual growth and health of members. These types of churches appeal to those who are searching.

The basis for this qualitative approach is the biblical illustration that a good tree produces good fruit (Matthew 7:17). Just as a tree that is healthy and strong produces fruit that is good to eat, a healthy, high-quality church produces members who are committed to Jesus and who are passionate about their faith. The addition of new members into the body is a side effect of this healthy "fruit." It is fascinating to see how well a statistical study demonstrates this biblical concept!

What Is the Weakest Area in Our Church?

Some Christians who hear these principles for the first time may wonder, "How am I supposed to think through all of this at once? I can't see the forest for the trees." This is the point where another outcome of the NCD study can be very helpful: to begin with, it is sufficient to concentrate on one single area. But which area?

It can be demonstrated that the growth of the church is blocked most by the quality characteristics which are least developed. However, this also means that if we concentrate our energy primarily on these minimum factors, we can expect that this alone can lead to growth.

It has been my experience that most Christians are not easily convinced of these church growth principles by well-reasoned, scientific analysis, but rather by a simple demonstration.

When I conducted NCD seminars, I had with me a barrel built with staves of varying lengths (see the picture on the next page). When the church showed me their church profile, I was able to show the results by writing the names of the eight quality characteristics on the staves according to how strongly or weakly each of the individual characteristics was developed. The name of the "minimum factor" was written on the shortest stave and the name of the maximum factor on the longest.

Then I poured water into the barrel until it overflowed. While pouring, the carpeting or the feet of those sitting

in the front row begin to get wet. I asked the participants, "What should I do?" Some, including the custodian, demanded that I stop pouring the water immediately. I did not, of course, because in this illustration the water symbolizes God's blessing flowing down from heaven into the church. We can't seriously ask God to stop blessing us just because our church has trouble "holding the water!"

Others suggested that we should pray more. While prayer is extremely important and absolutely essential for church growth, it must be followed with action. So I extended the longest stave, for example "passionate spirituality," four inches–and everyone could see that this noble measure did not solve the real problem. The water kept splashing on the floor.

Eventually someone would inevitably suggest that I lengthen the minimum factor stave. And look at that! As soon as that stave was lengthened–even just an inch–the barrel could hold more water. While this illustration may seem simplistic, it shows clearly that when it comes to the health of our churches, improving the lowest quality matters.

Our Work and God's Work

Such analogies demonstrate the central issues in church development. The barrel, composed of eight staves (e.g., quality characteristics) represents what we can and, according to God's will, should build. Admittedly, all our industrious improvements in the quality of the barrel cannot cause the water to flow into it. If God does not send water (that is, His blessings), even the finest barrel will stay dry. On the other hand, when God does pour out the water—and there is much theological evidence for the fact that He does so most willingly—then the quality of our "barrel" (church) is decisive. This quality ultimately determines whether the barrel can hold any water at all.

The apostle Paul may not use the picture of the barrel with staves, but he speaks of the same relationship between human and divine work when he uses the following words: "I planted the seed, Apollos watered it, but God made it grow" (1 Cor. 3:6, NIV). This clarifies what farmers already know, namely what they can "produce" and what they cannot. They can plant, water, and harvest, but they cannot make it grow; however, the farmers know that their planting and watering does influence the expected harvest.

Natural Church Development

The findings of research help us understand growth or decline in churches better. However, it is not enough to just understand. The best diagnosis is no good if the doctor does not offer any treatment.

To make sure that the discussion about church development does not end here, we have developed a series of resources to help with the practical implementation of the principles in the life of the church.

We call this approach to church growth that we have developed on the basis of our research "Natural Church Development." NCD America (NCDAmerica.org) is an agency established in 2016 to develop new and distribute existing NCD materials. (Inside the back cover you will find a few selected materials available through NCD America and the link to the online store.)

The NCD Cycle

The NCD Cycle in essence consists of three parts: the Test Phase, Plan Phase, and Experience Phase.

→ In the Test Phase, you assess your present starting point; this includes evaluating your own or your church's present state of fruitfulness.

→ In the <u>Plan Phase</u>, you focus your attention on what you have identified as a key area of need. This includes defining concrete action steps.

→ In the <u>Experience Phase</u>, you begin to live out what you have planned, including celebrating the fruit you see along the way.

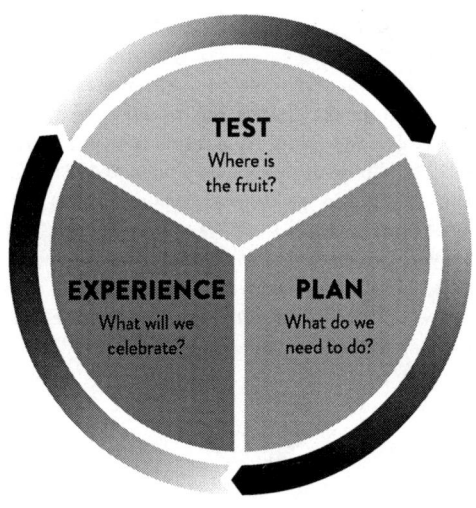

↑ The three basic steps in any development process: Test, Plan, and Experience.

The First Step

Many churches embark on Natural Church Development by first obtaining a church profile to identify the strengths and weaknesses of their church. The church profile answers, among other things, the question: Which of the eight quality characteristics is our current minimum factor?

To do this, 30 members (including the pastor) each fill out a questionnaire. The web site then analyzes the answers and compares them to the 19 million answers which we have collected so far. It then uses a special formula to calculate scores that are standardized based on a national norm. That is, the results are displayed in comparison to tens of thousands of other churches in the USA. The result serves as a basis to focus on the question: What can we do to experience growth in the area of our minimum factor? We hope, dear reader, that by now you can understand much better why this is a question that has true spiritual significance.

As we end, think again of the question Jesus asked: Do you (along with your church) want to get well?